BRITAIN IN OLD

AROUND BEVERLEY

PATRICIA E. DEANS &

JOHN MARKHAM

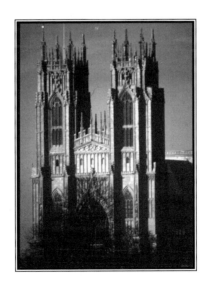

ALAN SUTTON PUBLISHING LIMITED

Alan Sutton Publishing Limited
Phoenix Mill · Far Thrupp · Stroud
Gloucestershire · GL5 2BU

First published 1995

Cover photographs: (front) Spencer School
annual orange distribution; (back) taking
'Great John' into the Minster.

British Library Cataloguing in Publication Data.
A catalogue record for this book is available from
the British Library.

ISBN 0-7509-0758-4

Typeset in 9/10 Sabon.
Typesetting and origination by
Alan Sutton Publishing Limited.
Printed in Great Britain by
Hartnolls, Bodmin, Cornwall.

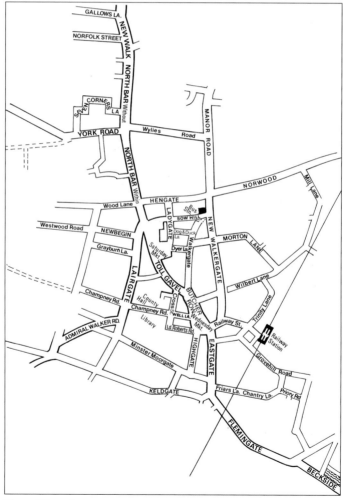

Plan of Beverley town centre.

Contents

Aerial view of Beverley looking south. The town developed northwards from the Minster area.

Introduction

This book looks at Beverley's past through the medium of photographs taken over the last 130 years, the period when, for the first time, we no longer have to speculate but can see for ourselves just what life was like. Ordinary scenes of everyday life of ordinary people doing everyday things have a particular fascination: they give an insight into a lost world which nothing can change, captured for ever on film.

Even where no photographs exist, Beverley is a town where evidence of the past is all around. Anyone who arrives by the road from York passes the fringe of trees on the outer edge of the Westwood; this is all that remains of the great forest which once reached to the town. From this higher ground you look ahead and see Beverley down in a hollow where water gathered and where beavers made their homes in the marshy terrain. The soaring western towers of the Minster dominate the skyline to the right, and, on the left, the beautifully proportioned tower of St Mary's rises gently above the roof tops.

This was a town where, in the Middle Ages, religion was an integral part of the life of the community. In AD 714 Bishop John of York came to Beverley to spend his last years in this quiet place surrounded by trees. The fame of his miracles spread and, after his canonization in 1037 as St John of Beverley, pilgrims journeyed in ever-increasing numbers to his tomb to seek his intercession. Pilgrims needed food, drink and shelter, as well as spiritual sustenance, and trade developed. Beverley's position by the River Hull gave it access to the Humber, the North Sea and Europe, and made it a port from which locally produced wool and cloth could be exported.

Beverley's markets and fairs grew in importance and attracted traders from distant parts. The town spread north and St Mary's had its origin as a chapel of ease for those who lived too far from the Minster to attend its services. It was this northern end of the town which was to become smart and prosperous with its own Saturday Market. This eclipsed the older market which had sprung up at the foot of the Minster and left the southern section of the town to its less glamorous but crucial role as the area which generated employment and wealth. As photographs show, the contrast was to have unexpected consequences this century when Armstrong Patents Co. Ltd expanded so phenomenally that its factory complex surrounded the Friary and reached almost to the Minster.

Beverley was never a walled town but it had an encircling ditch, and its four principal entrances were guarded by gates: only the North Bar survives. The gates were an inadequate defence against marauding armies and Beverley suffered at the hands of both Royalists and Parliamentarians in the Civil War. The Reformation had already had a serious impact on its important religious institutions, and clothmaking, the mainstay of its economy, was in terminal decline. Beverley was a town in the doldrums. It seemed that the great days had passed.

Human beings are resilient, however, and soon bounce back. Before the end of the seventeenth century Beverley was showing signs of the renaissance which was soon to transform its appearance. This change gives it that distinctive atmosphere which makes the town so attractive to residents and visitors today.

The Georgian period was a time of town improvement, so much so that the distinguished historian, K.A. MacMahon, could summarize these developments with no need to qualify his words: 'It is not too much to claim that the years of the eighteenth century saw the medieval character of the town radically altered.' Beverley became a miniature York where people of means resided or, if they were landed gentry, kept a town house. A theatre, assembly rooms and a racecourse catered for their social needs; a new Market Cross, a new Guildhall and an imposing Sessions House added to the dignity of the town; and pleasant, well-proportioned houses were built for the genteel private families who, as the visiting actor-manager, Tate Wilkinson, noted 'reside there in continuance'. Only a handful of the timber-framed houses which were once so plentiful in Beverley survive, although a building's Georgian appearance is sometimes only skin-deep and the original structure is concealed beneath the cosmetic façade.

Two well-appointed coaching inns, the Beverley Arms and the Tiger, provided hospitality for well-off travellers, and the comments made by those who came compensate in some way for the absence of photographs. 'A pretty idle town', observed James Boswell, biographer of Dr Johnson, in 1778, and, although it was raining heavily when she passed through in 1802, Dorothy Wordsworth was 'much pleased with the beauty of the town'.

The Beverley which emerges from the early photographs is a small country town with a strong sense of community. A number of buildings in the centre have been Victorianized and look grander than their Georgian predecessors, but there were no particularly large stores; instead, an enviable variety of small shops. These were usually staffed by the proprietors and their families, and goods were home-made, specially tailored or appropriately shaped, and supplied with the prompt and courteous service their demanding customers expected.

Public events brought people of all ages out into the streets, into Saturday Market and to the Westwood to share the fun which was all the more enjoyable for being free. People not only lived but also worked in the town, usually in small businesses, although menacing signs of change were on the horizon. Beverley's traditional trades developed into large-scale industries, and for a time the town itself was overtaken by William Crosskill's agricultural engineering firm which, at its peak, employed 800 men. If it had not been stopped in its tracks by a financial crisis, it might have created a very different Beverley from the one that remains.

As in other places, the motor car's impact on the town was eventually to prove a serious threat to Beverley's narrow streets. On the other side of the coin, the car was also the means of generating work and wealth with the advent of Armstrong Patents Co. Ltd, manufacturers of shock absorbers.

A town is a living entity and has to keep pace with changing circumstances. New roads have had to be built and new buildings erected. Controversy has at times been intense, but anyone who looks through the pages of this book will see that, though many things have gone, much remains. Recording Beverley's past may help to encourage optimism about its future.

Section One

A WALK THROUGH
THE TOWN

Beverley, looking south, c. 1890. The tall chimney on the left, a feature in many old photographs of the town, belonged to Stephenson's Golden Ball Brewery in Walkergate, behind its Toll Gavel public house. The brewery was rebuilt in 1869 and closed in 1919 after Robert Stephenson's death. Note the number of trees.

The Minster and Eastgate from the north-east, *c.* 1860. Thomas Crump's woodyard, in the foreground, was part of Tindall's 130-acre nursery garden. It was occupied by Crosskill's works from 1864 to 1914 and afterwards by Armstrong Patents until 1981.

The Minster from the station. Armstrong Patents' massive development was incongruously close to the church. The flower displays in the foreground are in the station gardens and frequently won prizes.

View from Cartwright Lane to the Minster across a still rural area. It was transformed by housing before and after the Second World War.

View from The Hall, Lairgate, to the Minster. Work has already started on developing the former estate of Rear Admiral Charles F. Walker, the last private resident of The Hall. He died in 1925 and his house and land were bought by Beverley Borough Council in 1926.

The large orchard is bordered by Minster Moorgate (bottom right), St John Street (bottom left), Keldgate (centre) and Lairgate (top right). St Martin's and St Matthew's Courts were built here in 1985–87. A workhouse for the parishes of St Martin, St Mary and St Nicholas was erected on part of this site *c.* 1726. It had its frontage towards Minster Moorgate. When the Georgian guildhall was being built in 1762, members of the Corporation met in the workhouse. In 1849 ten inmates died of cholera. It was demolished in 1861 when the Union Workhouse was built near the Westwood.

The Highgate approach to the Minster. Just visible to the left is a characteristic Beverley cottage with dormer windows and sliding sashes.

Highgate Pump. The handsome cast-iron water pump formerly stood on the east side of Highgate. In 1891 there were over 300 public and private pumps in Beverley. When Celia Fiennes, the famous diarist, visited Beverley in 1697, she was impressed by the number of wells surrounded by walls from which water could be drawn by buckets operated by a system of pulley and weights. Most were later converted to pumps.

United service at the Minster, Friday 20 May 1910. The service was to mourn the death of Edward VII and was held at 1 p.m. It was timed to coincide with the funeral at Windsor. Seating was provided for 3,000 people and crowds were waiting for the opening of the doors for over an hour before the service began. The vicar, Canon H.E. Nolloth, was fulsome in his praise of the late king as a religious man, but felt obliged to defend him from unpleasant rumours: 'Credulous is the man who believes one hundredth part of the idle tales which gain currency concerning the great.'

Dismantling the tall wall round the Minster and its replacement with iron railings, 1905. Canon H.E. Nolloth, the long-serving vicar, 1880–1921, was responsible for many improvements to the Minster.

The east end of the Minster can be seen on the left. On the extreme right is the timber-framed building (see pages 65, 66); in the background, the Sun Inn.

Beverley was described in the sixteenth century as a town 'well builded of wood'. This fine late fifteenth-century timbered house, 6–8 Highgate, survived until it was demolished in 1956. It has since been replaced with modern houses.

The end of Highgate at its junction with Wednesday Market. The timber-framed house is on the left, and on the opposite side are typical Beverley cottages, also now demolished.

Wednesday Market, pre-1909. Lord Roberts Road was opened in 1909: its construction involved demolishing part of Highgate House, built in the eighteenth century. The house numbered some distinguished doctors among its former residents and featured in J.S. Fletcher's novel *The House in Tuesday Market*.

Wednesday Market, *c.* 1910. This, the town's oldest market area, had long been superseded by Saturday Market and its character altered by the opening of Railway Street in 1846 and Lord Roberts Road in 1909.

Wednesday Market, looking north. Just visible through the trees is the shop of D.H. Witty, printer. On the right is the Primitive Methodist Chapel, built in 1868. It was replaced by, first, Crystal Garage, and in 1994 by Boyes. To its right, almost in the centre of the picture, is B.L. Ramshaw, pork butcher and beer retailer.

Wednesday Market, looking north, post-1916. On the left is 21 Wednesday Market where Benjamin Ramshaw combined his trade of pork butcher with running the Spotted Cow, a beer-house. As the notice shows, he also sold sandwiches – presumably pork! On the right of the photograph is 3 Wednesday Market, the shop of John Henry Leighton, greengrocer. The Marble Arch cinema, opened in 1916, advertises its programme in the background.

Wednesday Market, looking towards Butcher Row, 1910. The congregation of the Primitive Methodist Chapel are leaving the service on Sunday, probably on 8 May 1910, after the death of Edward VII.

Wednesday Market, 1899. This is probably Barnum and Bailey's spectacular – and free! – circus procession to advertise the performance on 8 August. On the extreme left in each photograph is J.H. Leighton's greengrocer's shop, then John Musson's boot and shoe shop and, next to that, the Queen's Head (with sign). The tall chimney belongs to the Eastgate factory which began as William Crosskill & Sons and became the East Yorkshire and Crosskills Cart and Waggon Co.

Another view of the procession, Butcher Row. William Tilson's stationer's shop is on the left, and, in the background, the Golden Ball Brewery chimney.

Butcher Row, late 1800s. An opportunity to be photographed was not to be missed.

Butcher Row, looking north-east. The late nineteenth-century single-storey shop is that of James Horner, photographer. The well-known firm of house furnishers, Gresswells, later occupied 25–29 Butcher Row on this side.

33–39 Butcher Row, *c.* 1912. The children are standing outside timber-framed buildings, some of which are medieval and some of seventeenth-century date. After their demolition the Marble Arch cinema was built here and opened on 14 September 1916. It took its name from the passage known locally by that name.

Butcher Row. A later photograph showing the demolition or natural decay of the house in front of which the children were standing (see above).

School Lane, Walkergate. This led to the now-demolished school which was opened in 1844. It was originally Wesleyan, but was taken over by the local authority in 1905 and renamed Spencer School in honour of its long-serving headmaster, Alderman William Spencer. He served there for thirty-nine years from 1848 to 1887.

Spencer Street, Walkergate. Originally Duncumb Street, it was renamed in 1881, also in honour of William Spencer (see above).

Toll Gavel (left) and Walkergate (right). The pump adjacent to the shop window on the right was known as Prison Pump because it stood near the former town prison, which was demolished in about 1811. Its outline can still be seen on the wall.

Toll Gavel, further north. On the extreme right is the eighteenth-century house which belonged to Anne Routh, a great benefactress of Beverley, who in 1722 left her estates to found the almshouse in Keldgate which bears her name. Next to it is the Oddfellows' Hall. The proprietor of the draper's shop on the left was Uriah Butters, who took many photographs of Beverley at the end of the nineteenth century.

Toll Gavel, Butcher Row and Walkergate corner, 24 July 1912. A cloudburst created never-to-be-forgotten floods, and the culverted Walker Beck, which ran along Walkergate, overflowed.

Toll Gavel, looking towards Butcher Row. An era ends as stone setts are replaced by tarmacadam.

The Holderness Hunt entering Toll Gavel, 28 December 1909. Scales & Son Ltd, on the right, were bootmakers. This building, 1 Toll Gavel, is now occupied by Burtons.

Holderness Hunt in Toll Gavel, 28 December 1909. The hounds had met for the first time for many years in Saturday Market. A shoot on the Westwood resulted in the hunt taking this route to Bentley. The *Beverley Independent*, on the far right, was at 53 Toll Gavel.

Toll Gavel, *c.* 1906. A knife-grinder's machine stands outside Mrs E. Copley's pork shop on the left. Later she moved to 13 Butcher Row. The large building half-way down on the right with the hanging lamp is the Holderness Hotel; to its right is Robert Haylock's boot shop.

The Holderness Hotel, Toll Gavel. Formerly the Blue Boar, it had £500 spent on it in 1829 and was given the new name to mark its upgrading. It had stabling for sixty horses. In Beverley's keenly fought nineteenth-century parliamentary elections it was frequented by Liberals. Later it became Schofield's shop.

Toll Gavel, *c.* 1900. At the turn of the century it was a busy street but still not overcrowded with traffic. Note the gas lighting: it was first installed in Beverley streets in 1824.

Saturday Market, *c*. 1863. The shop on the far left was that of J. Wilson, hatter. It was given a much grander appearance when it was rebuilt by architect William Hawe in 1863. For many years it was occupied by George Hobson, grocer, before being taken over by the Midland Bank *c*. 1910.

63 Saturday Market, *c*. 1863. This is another view of Mr Wilson's hat shop (see previous picture).

Corn Hill, Saturday Market, c. 1885. Carriers' carts brought in goods, and sometimes passengers, from the villages around. Corn was sold in this area as early as the fourteenth century and it was known as Corn Hill by the seventeenth century. The first Corn Exchange was built in 1825.

Saturday Market, c. 1938. East Yorkshire Motor Services continued to use the market area for buses until the Sow Hill coach station was developed in the late 1960s. In the background can just be seen the changed façade of no. 63 (see previous page).

Saturday Market, west side. In the late nineteenth century much grander buildings replaced most of the neat and simple Georgian shops. One survives here, no. 55, the fourth on the right. It was Thomas Burton's boot shop.

Saturday Market, looking south, *c.* 1885. Farm produce was sold directly from carts in this area, which was known as Butter Dings by the eighteenth century. The range of shops on the left was built in 1775.

Saturday Market, pre-1939. The surface is part cobbles, part tarmacadam. Parking was no problem! Burtons, the outfitters, had not yet occupied its corner site with its frontage on Toll Gavel: the trade name appeared for the first time in a Beverley town directory in 1939.

Saturday Market, immediately pre- or post-war. There is more traffic but East Yorkshire Motor Services still use the area for buses.

Sow Hill, Saturday Market, *c.* 1900. The shops are (left to right): John Smith, wine and spirits; Hephzibah Beaulah, dairy; G.W. Almond, tailor; J.W. Laughton, butcher; M. Smith, grocer; Arnott & Sons, drapers.

Saturday Market, Corn Hill. Mills and Sowerby's wine and spirits shop had previously been a chemist's. It became Ernest Mills' in the 1930s and is now the Push Inn, at last known officially by the colloquial name derived from a sign on the door.

The Corn Exchange, built in 1886, which replaced the earlier Georgian exchange. As well as selling corn, it was used for a short period as a temporary school until Walkergate School was completed in 1906. In 1911 it became a cinema. The first performance was on 20 February of that year: regular performances began in March. Soon after, it was renamed the Picture Playhouse but continued to be used for sales of corn until 1947. Patrons remember brushing seeds off their cinema seats.

THE

Picture

Playhouse.

MARKET	TWICE NIGHTLY,	BEVER-
PLACE,	7 and 9	LEY.

THE POPULAR AND COSY HOUSE OF ENTERTAINMENT.

High Class PROGRAMMES and Distinctive

Some very Big Productions have been booked for the Winter Season.
☞ FOR DETAILS WATCH OUR DAY BILLS. ☜

POPULAR PRICES.   ORCHESTRAL MUSIC.

RESERVE SEATS CAN BE BOOKED.
Box Office 'Phone 15 Beverley.

Saturday Market, entrance to Dyer Lane. The crowds are possibly spectators leaving a meet of the Holderness Hunt – certainly one of the popular public events.

The Globe Inn, Ladygate, *c.* 1910. Although an inn where travellers put up their horse-drawn vehicles, its resources were stretched when an elephant was lodged there. The animal was probably part of Bostock and Wombwell's Travelling Zoo which visited Beverley on 17 October 1910 (also on 16 October 1908). The Globe was demolished when Sow Hill was opened up in 1968.

Too humble to be named! The quaint and atmospheric back lane behind the buildings in Butter Dings, Saturday Market, was known simply as Playhouse Passage, because of the nearby cinema. It may have been the unidentified medieval Pudding Lane.

Harry Dale's fish and chip shop, 35 Ladygate. This was a new type of fast food business and looks rather out of place in such a historic street. The man at the door is probably the proud proprieter.

The proclamation of George V from the Market Cross, 11 May 1910. It was read by the new Mayor-elect, Richard Care, as the elected Mayor, William H. Elwell had just died in office. Care was the first mayor in England to be sworn in under George V.

Military procession, Saturday Market, 15 February 1902. The occasion was the unveiling in the Minster of a memorial window to men of the East Yorkshire Regiment who had died in the Boer War.

A memorable Sunday, 7 July 1907. Beverley became a military town after the opening of the Victoria Barracks in 1877. Over 800 men marched to the Minster in the morning, and, in the afternoon, the members of Friendly Societies processed to St Mary's Church.

Kemp's Corner. John Kemp's well-known printing business on a prominent site at the junction of Saturday Market and Lairgate meant that Beverlonians always referred to this point by its unofficial name, Kemp's Corner. The premises were demolished in 1968 to allow road widening. As well as producing masses of leaflets and posters for Beverley's keenly fought parliamentary elections in the mid-nineteenth century, Kemp was also a newsagent, bookseller, stationer and newspaper proprietor. Latterly the site was Duncan Simson's photographic and pet shop.

St Mary's Church. Flying buttresses were added to the south transept (right) and the turrets on the west front (left) were replaced by the eminent Victorian architects, A.W.N. Pugin and E.W. Pugin during restorations from 1844 to 1852.

North Bar Within, 1930s. Always a smart area, it retained its dignified atmosphere with ample parking space and no yellow lines.

Beverley Arms, North Bar Within. Originally the Blue Bell, it had been rebuilt and re-named the Beverley Arms in 1794. It was owned by the Morley family from 1852 to 1920. Arthur R. Jebson's butcher's shop (left of the hotel) was demolished for neo-Georgian extensions in 1967.

Beverley Arms: election night fever. A. Stanley Wilson, Conservative MP for Holderness 1900–1922 (the constituency then included Beverley), always used the hotel as his headquarters. He held his seat in a Liberal landslide in 1906 by thirty votes, but lost it in 1922 when the first Labour government was elected.

Tiger Lane, North Bar Within. The lane took its name from the former Tiger Inn, an important coaching inn from 1730 to 1847. After closure it was divided into shops and, by 1929, John Ellis Hopper occupied one of them. On the opposite corner of the lane is one of Beverley's last surviving timbered buildings, probably fifteenth century in date. It is now part of St Mary's Court, opened in 1983.

North Bar Within, *c.* 1877. The house on the right was demolished some time before 1910. To its left, beyond Coombs Yard, was the King's Arms. This is now shops, although the iron bracket of the inn sign survives.

North Bar Within. An unusual feature of this smart area of Beverley was the relatively brief conversion of the last of the Georgian terraced houses on the left, next to Bar House, into a fish shop.

North Bar, July 1910. It was reported in the *Beverley Guardian* that the Bar had been closed for three days from 23 July, for the first time within living memory, to enable road repairs to be undertaken. The fifteenth-century Bar is the only surviving one of the four which stood at principal roads into Beverley. It is now usually kept open, but is closed and then opened on ceremonial occasions when a regiment honoured with the Freedom of Beverley is formally admitted to the town.

North Bar, 22 June 1897. The occasion was probably the sports on the Westwood held as part of Queen Victoria's Diamond Jubilee celebrations, 22 June 1897. Here the crowds are returning. Festivities began with a ball (21 June), continued with a procession to the Minster, sports and dinner for old people (22 June) and ended with a children's ball (23 June).

North Bar, floodlit. The grand occasion was the Diamond Jubilee celebrations, 21–23 June 1897, when public buildings in the town were illuminated (see previous photograph).

North Bar – a tight squeeze. East Yorkshire Motor Services needed specially designed gothic-roofed buses to pass through the North Bar. Even so, a bus driver had to negotiate the narrow throughway with great accuracy and there were a number of mishaps over the years. Buses ceased to use the North Bar in 1983.

North Bar, *c.* 1866. Bar House on the right was given its present appearance in 1866, after this photograph was taken. The western pedestrian way through the Bar was constructed around 1867.

North Bar Without. The demolition of shops on the far left allowed the Rose and Crown to acquire a forecourt and to move the main entrance from its former position on York Road. The Catholic Church of St John of Beverley, right of the Rose and Crown, had its first service on Christmas Day 1897. The sign-post on the right points to York.

York Road. Shops stood at the corner, and the main entrance of the Rose and Crown was in York Road. It was a Georgian inn but had been Victorianized and was later to be given its present mock-Tudor appearance.

Wylies Road. A rare, possibly unique, picture of the western end of what is now a principal thoroughfare but which was merely a lane until around 1960. The road took its name from Robert Wylie, who formerly occupied the now demolished house on the right.

The Elms, North Bar Without. Built *c*. 1730–40 by William Wrightson, this is one of the many fine Georgian buildings which give Beverley its distinctive character. The stable block (left) was replaced by late Victorian houses.

New Walk. Laid out as a fashionable tree-lined promenade in the 1780s, it was far more spacious and attractive for strollers than the cobbled town streets with narrow – or no – footpaths. The chestnut trees date from 1822 and, although some fine houses were built, the road retained its rural aspect until the late nineteenth century.

Sessions House, New Walk, built 1805–10. It not only provided accommodation for courts of law but was also used for county business and for the formal aspects of parliamentary elections. A large crowd awaits the declaration of the result in the period before mass communications, when political events attracted huge attendances.

Molescroft Road. This remained a rural road in the late nineteenth century, before it had developed as a major – and fashionable – residential area. The house (right) was Elmsall Lodge, built c. 1880 by Henry Dixon, in business as a silk merchant in Hull. Later it became the home of Harry Wray, solicitor and civic leader.

Beverley Library, Champney Road. The original section of the building was erected in 1906 at the expense of J.E. Champney, on land given by William Spencer.

Baptist Chapel, Well Lane, looking towards Cross Street, pre-1909. The chapel was demolished in 1909 so that Lord Roberts Road could be cut through. The last service was held on 21 March 1909. To the left is 11 Cross Street, built in about 1834, and occupied in 1909 by George Ford.

Demolition of the Baptist Chapel, Well Lane, 1909. The view is past the front of the building along Well Lane.

The YMCA hut which stood at the corner of Lord Roberts Road. This was opposite the former clinic and was used by the St John Ambulance nurses at weekends. Pleasant gardens now occupy the site.

Laying the foundation stones of the new Baptist Chapel, Lord Roberts Road, 8 July 1909. A distinguished gathering included the resident minister, the Revd W.H. Davies, and the mayor and mayoress, Councillor and Mrs R. Care. Nine foundation stones were laid, the first by Mrs Payne, whose father, Mr Johnston, was the first Baptist minister in Beverley.

Newbegin, c. 1900. These Beverley cottages, with dormer windows and sliding sashes, have now been demolished.

A street party, Princes Gardens. The party is possibly to celebrate the coronation in 1937.

Eastgate, looking south. The southern end of Eastgate has not yet been widened and the Victorian extension of the Minster vicarage (extreme left of the row of houses) not yet demolished. The widening took place in the early 1960s.

Eastgate, looking north. The old vicarage is just visible on the left. The end of the former Sun Inn (now the Tap and Spile) is on the extreme right.

Friary doorway, Eastgate. To save a sixteenth-century doorway of the Dominican Friary from demolition, as Armstrong Patents developed its site, it was transferred across the road to the old vicarage wall on 14 June 1964.

Minster Moorgate. A characteristic row of neat Georgian cottages replaced buildings that were once part of the Minster complex.

Fox's Hospital, Minster Moorgate, pre-1890. This row of almshouses, given by Thwaites Fox in 1636 for the use of four poor widows, was demolished in 1890 to make way for Jubilee Terrace.

Hebb Brothers' garage, 87–89 Lairgate. The absence of heavy traffic made the early years of the century a golden age for cycling.

Procession passing The Hall, Lairgate, *c.* 1904. The Hall was then the home of Rear Admiral Charles Walker, its last private resident, who died in 1925.

Lairgate. The wall on the right enclosed The Hall's garden. Parts are still visible opposite the Tiger and among houses built on the former estate.

Lairgate, northern end, *c.* 1904. St Mary's Church is in the background.

Keldgate. The cottage stood at the Keldgate end of the path (marked by the posts) known as the Leases.

The Leases. This quiet path, with the town ditch to its right, was developed for housing in the 1930s.

From the Leases looking across the town ditch and a paddock on The Hall estate. This central but still rural area was developed for housing in 1926–30.

Albert Terrace. The town ditch, which continued along this line, had to be infilled so that the Victorian houses could be built. The building on the left, which became the fire station and is now a clinic, opened as the Foundation School in 1861.

Keldgate viewed from Cartwright Lane. Keldgate Bar, which stood near this point, was demolished in 1808. Victoria Road is on the right, and on the corner are almshouses donated by Elizabeth Westoby in 1863.

Keldgate. Outside no. 29 is the so-called 'stone dog' (extreme right of the photograph). The origin of the 'dog' is unknown but it may have come from the demolished Keldgate Bar or St Thomas' Chapel not far away.

The 'stone dog'. One suggestion is that the animal was a 'sea dog' or beaver, the symbol of Beverley. The stone monument was rescued by Mr T.A. Lazenby and given by him to stand in the grounds of the Friary.

Keldgate, near its junction with Lairgate, pre-1890. The end of the Georgian grammar school, demolished in 1890, can be seen on the extreme right.

Keldgate, approaching the Minster. Note the number of trees in the churchyard. Beverley was always noted for its trees.

Keldgate, junction with Long Lane. The old cottages in the centre of the picture were demolished at the turn of the century.

Keldgate, east end. Houses have now replaced the cottages on the left. The soldiers may be marching from the barracks to the Minster.

Cabs waiting outside Beverley station. The line from Hull to Bridlington, with buildings designed by G.T. Andrews, opened on 6 October 1846. It was linked to Scarborough in 1847.

Station Square viewed from the railway station. An impressive but unidentifiable Edwardian event attracts the crowds. The kiosk on the right was the cabbies' shelter. In the background on the left is Railway Street, built around 1849 as a grand avenue leading to the new railway station.

Flemingate. The timber-framed building which stood opposite the Sun Inn (note its sign on the extreme left) may have been part of the Minster complex.

The timber-framed building (see photograph above) viewed from the north-east, showing its proximity to the east end of the Minster.

Flemingate, *c.* 1912. This building (see previous page) was demolished in 1912 and replaced by Constitution Hall, which in turn has been replaced by modern housing.

Flemingate. There is a tradition that the brick-built house on the extreme right was the birthplace of St John Fisher. It dates only from 1660–70, however, and Fisher was executed in 1535.

THE BECK AND THE SHIPYARD

Beverley Beck. The Beck, a canalized section of the River Hull, has been described as the town's lifeline before the coming of the railway. Beckside was Beverley's port area and industry gravitated to this southern part of the town where goods and materials could be transported by water.

Beckside scenes. Buildings by the side of a waterway give this part of Beverley a Dutch atmosphere. In spite of its tranquil appearance the Beck placed Beverley on an international route by giving it access to the North Sea and so to Europe. A lock was built in 1802–3, at the confluence of the Beck and the River Hull, and in the nineteenth century tanning, milling and shipbuilding in the area became important factors in the town's prosperity.

The lock seen from the River Hull entry. In the background on the right is the area later occupied by Deans and Son (Yorkshire) Ltd. The lock-keeper's cottage is in the centre.

A Humber keel. The square-sailed Humber keels were the main vessels sailing to and from Beverley. Here one is seen on the River Hull.

Watersports, 11 September 1897. These are always a crowd-puller. They are not on the Beck, as is sometimes stated, but, as the banks indicate, on the River Hull.

Shipyards, c. 1900. The demand for steam trawlers encouraged the expansion of shipbuilding, a traditional Beverley industry, by such firms as Cook, Welton and Gemmell on the west bank of the river and Joseph Scarr on the east.

The shipyard on the west bank of the river. In the background is the Nags Head. Workmen gather round a steam pump in action, probably newly acquired.

The building of the *W.A. Massey*, 1895. She was a steam trawler and was built on the west bank of the River Hull. The yard concentrated on building trawlers for the Hull and Grimsby fleets.

Necessity is the mother of invention. The narrow River Hull was hardly ideal for shipbuilding and this photograph, taken in about 1905, shows the spectacular sideways launch which had to be adopted.

Launch of the *Kingston Comet*, 1950.

Weel ferry. The floating bridge to Weel sank in 1949 and people had to revert to the old way of crossing the river – by ferry – until 1953 when a new bridge was built at Grovehill.

Opening of the new Weel Bridge, 19 October 1953. Cook, Welton and Gemmell were commissioned to build a bridge to replace the inconvenient ferry and it was formally opened by the Mayor, Councillor C.P. Dunn.

The end of an era. Difficult economic and political circumstances, the advent of deep-sea trawlers too large to be built in Beverley, as well as the Cod War, had a disastrous effect on the town's shipyards. The *C.S. Forester*, launched in May 1969, was the last of the Beverley trawlers.

Section Three

INDUSTRIES –
LARGE AND SMALL

Long Lane. Beverley's minor industries in the nineteenth century included the building of

small carriages and carts. This is a governess car (or cart) built by E.W. and G. Osgerby

of Highgate (see next page).

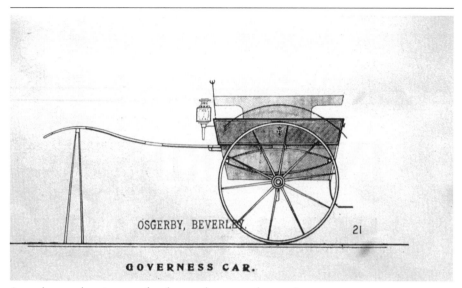

A catalogue advertisement for the car shown on the previous page.

A smart turn-out in Osgerby's Highgate yard.

Hodgson's tannery, Flemingate. The business, established by William Hodgson in 1812, had grown into a large-scale industry. In 1920 the company was taken over by Barrow, Hepburn and Gale, but difficult circumstances caused its substantial closure in 1978.

Hodgson's tannery. Fleshing (scraping) hides. This photograph, and those overleaf, were taken in the late 1950s.

Hodgson's tannery. Setting out (trimming) shoulders.

Hodgson's tannery. Drying shed for machine belting and for upholstery leather.

The small non-ferrous foundry of Deans and Son (Yorkshire) Ltd, a family engineering firm. Founded in Hull in 1905, it moved to Beverley in 1925, taking over a large part of Pennock Tigar's works, where paint, whiting and fertilizers had been manufactured. It was first engaged in manufacturing musical instruments but, following the 1930s' slump, it branched out into public transport fittings.

Deans' machine shop during the Second World War. At this time machinery was driven by belt and shafting from a large central engine.

Deans' nickel-plating shop.

The home front. During the Second World War factories had their own firefighting teams and took very seriously competitions to demonstrate operational efficiency. This is Deans' team practising beside the River Hull: the shipyard is in the background.

'The Gordon', *c.* 1909. It was named after its inventor. The firm, which became Armstrong Patents Co. Ltd and played a crucial role in the town's twentieth-century history, was founded in 1907 by Gordon Armstrong when he opened a garage and workshop in North Bar Within. In 1909 he produced this car.

Gordon Armstrong (centre) – the aviator. In 1910 he took to the air for the first and last time. He flew from the Westwood in a second-hand aircraft into which he had fitted a 25 h.p. Anzani engine.

Armstrong Patents' Eastgate Office, built 1937 and demolished *c*. 1964. Armstrong Patents' prosperity was largely based on the manufacture of shock absorbers for the motor industry, producing the first in 1919 on the site Gordon Armstrong had acquired in Eastgate.

Armstrong Patents' factory. By 1960 the factory employed around two thousand people.

Section Four

AROUND THE TOWN

Walkergate, c. 1890. The area developed in medieval times along the winding route of the
Walker Beck where cloth was 'walked' in the cleaning and thickening process. In the late
nineteenth century Walkergate was a densely populated residential area mostly of modest
houses. This view looks towards the Assembly Rooms which, in 1935, became the Regal
cinema. Road widening in the 1960s considerably altered the northern end and, since 1980,
it has been known as Old Walkergate to distinguish it from its younger counterpart.

St Mary's House, Hengate. It was the residence of Clive Wilson, the son of Arthur Wilson of Tranby Croft. On 29 December 1912 it was damaged in a serious fire and Wilson never rebuilt it. The ruins were demolished and Wilson gave the site to the town in 1917: it is now part of the Memorial Gardens.

Timber-framed buildings in (Old) Walkergate. They were demolished when Sow Hill bus station was built in the late 1960s.

Neville Avenue, *c.* 1923. Beverley Borough Council used government grants to help buy land in Grovehill Road in 1920. Three years later eighty-six concrete-built houses had been completed, among them these in Neville Avenue.

Swinemoor Lane at its junction with Grovehill Road, *c.* 1900. The two large houses, and one not shown, were built by Joseph Scarr and Sons Ltd, shipbuilders, for members of the Scarr family.

Norwood House, view from the garden. Built in about 1760 for attorney Jonathan Midgley, it had a number of interesting occupants before being purchased by the East Riding County Council and opened in 1908 as Beverley High School for Girls.

The North Eastern Railway Company introduced a bus service between Beverley railway station and Beeford on 7 September 1903. Two vehicles were in use and there were four journeys in each direction daily. The total time for each journey was one hour 50 minutes.

Section Five

SHOPS

Clark and Botham's fish shop, 11 North Bar Within. The door of the modern shop is on the left, not central. Robert Henry Clark and Percy Botham ran this business from the mid-1920s into the postwar period.

Percy Whiting's well-stocked grocery shop, 5 North Bar Within. More recently this became Ray Hawley's antique shop and is now the Beverley offices of the *Hull Daily Mail*. In the early years of the century Beverley was a town of small shopkeepers.

Saturday Market. Shops in the eighteenth-century buildings on Butter Dings (left to right): Robert Mayman, saddler; Alfred Tiplady, hairdresser; Rutherford's Refreshment Rooms; Akrill's gun shop (still recognizable); Thos. Drewery, china.

C.A. Skinner's saddler's shop, 64 Saturday Market. Presumably the name of the proprietor, Thomas Clowes, there in the 1870s, was worth retaining. This and the adjacent shop, Abraham Altham Ltd, tea dealers, have been replaced by the TSB.

Saturday Market, *c.* 1897. A carter delivers grain or flour to Gilbert Dove and Son, corn and provision merchants. To the left is Henry Schofield, tailor and clothier, who was later to move into Toll Gavel. At the far left is Green's, printers, stationers and publishers of the *Beverley Guardian*. On the right is Christiana Fenwick, haberdasher and seller of Berlin wool (thread used for worsted embroidery) and fancy goods.

M. Smith, grocer, 6 Saturday Market, standing at the door of his shop. Although he showed no great artistic skill in his window display, some of the signs and containers would now be valuable collectors' items.

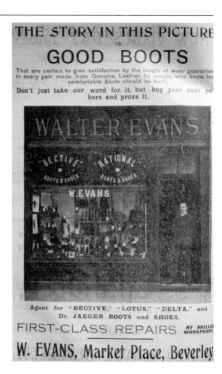

Walter Evans, boot and shoe shop, 58
Saturday Market.

James Nelson, butcher, 10 Toll Gavel. He moved here from 23 Wednesday Market in
about 1910. Next door at 8 Toll Gavel is James Morley's drugs store.

Maypole Dairy, 22 Toll Gavel. This is at the right-hand corner of Landress Lane.

WE SPECIALIZE

in

High-class

MEN'S

WEAR

at

Most Moderate Prices.

We value your Enquiries.

18 & 20,

BUTCHER ROW,

BEVERLEY.

Arthur Peabody, gents' outfitter, 18–20 Butcher Row (now Brookes).

R. WALGATE = = Tailor = =

National Telephone 127.   36 Toll Gavel, BEVERLEY.

SUITS FOR ALL
OCCASIONS.

Ordinary, Everyday
Wear.

Dress Suits for
Evening Wear.

Norfolk and Flannel
Suits for
Holiday Wear.

Riding Breeches.

Clerical Garments.

Motoring Outfits.

Liveries.

SPECIALISTS IN
LADIES'
TAILORING.

Coats and Skirts
correct in every
detail.

Perfect Fitting
Riding Habits.

ALL ORDERS CAREFULLY AND PROMPTLY ATTENDED TO.

Ralph Walgate, tailor, 36 Toll Gavel.

Gresswell and Co., house furnishers, 25–29 Butcher Row. One of Beverley's larger stores, the firm began in 1914 as F.W. Gresswell, watchmaker, at 27 Butcher Row. By the 1920s it had expanded into adjacent premises. Both buildings were demolished at the same time as the Marble Arch cinema, in 1967, and the site is now occupied by a supermarket.

Marble Arch cinema. Rather surprisingly it was built in the middle of the First World War in 1916. It had a seating capacity of 1,100 people. It closed in 1967 and was demolished to make way for a supermarket.

VIOLET HUNT

High-class Ladies' Outfitter

WEDNESDAY MARKET, BEVERLEY

Violet Hunt's ladies' fashion shop. This was situated at the corner of Railway Street (to the left) and Eastgate. A substantial private residence in the early nineteenth century, the building was later converted into N.J. Gray's grocer's shop. The mock-Tudor porch had been added earlier than 1892 and, after a long period as Violet Hunt's, it became the Tudor Rose restaurant.

Jaeger Under and Outer Wear   J.B. Corsets
Valstar Weather Coats   Dent's Gloves, etc.

John Musson's Boots and Shoes, Wednesday Market, with the Musson family in the doorway. Situated at the corner of Tindall Lane, it is now Jackson and Dufton, estate agents.

Harry Wharton Brough's grocer's shop in Highgate. He also had a shop at 19 Butcher Row and, at one time, another in Lairgate.

William Fawcett, greengrocer, 7 Wednesday Market. Mr and Mrs Fawcett, seen here, were the proud proprietors of a shop with an impressive frontage and a well-stocked window display. Note that no respectable man would be seen outside without a hat or cap. It is now H. Peck and Son's fish shop.

Section Six

SCHOOLS

St Mary's National School, Cross Street, celebrating Empire

Day in front of County Hall, c. 1910. The school (just

visible, extreme right), built 1849, was popularly known as

'Square School' because of its location in what was then part

of Register Square. Empire Day, 24 May, was the

anniversary of Queen Victoria's birthday and an occasion for

great patriotic celebrations. Extensions to County Hall,

shown here, (right background) were completed in 1908.

Queen Victoria's Diamond Jubilee celebrations, Corn Hill, Saturday Market, 24 June 1897. More than 3,000 Beverley schoolchildren joined in the national celebrations but on a day after the main events were over. After presentation of medals the children marched to Saturday Market where they sang *Rule Britannia* and the National Anthem before enjoying sports, games, buns and cheesecakes on the Westwood.

The same occasion. In the background are the buildings on the east side of Saturday Market. Dyer Lane and the Pack Horse are left of centre. To the right is the King's Head.

Minster Infants School marching to the Diamond Jubilee presentation, 1897. Nearing the end of a long walk from Flemingate, the 'crocodile' is moving along Toll Gavel with Butcher Row in the background and Cross Street to the right.

Minster Infants School, Flemingate. The school opened in 1852, was enlarged in 1871 and closed in 1914. Note the disciplined rows of pupils, the absence of distracting windows and the numbers taught in one large room.

Beverley Grammar School, Queensgate. In 1902 the school moved to this new building from the former Foundation School in Albert Terrace. The Edwardian building still stands near the entrance to the school ground.

Beverley Grammar School 1st XI Football Team, 1920. Back row, left to right: G. Sole de Neal (master), T.R. Appleton, T. Haller, W. Scott, E. Witty. Middle row: C.F. Deans, ? Stephenson, T. Clappison. Front row: J. Johnson, J. Taylor, F.W. Gresswell, ? Richmond, ? Simpson.

Spencer Council School orange distribution. Opened as a Wesleyan day school in 1840, it moved to School Lane in 1844. It was taken over by the local authority in 1905 and renamed in honour of Alderman William Spencer, the distinguished long-serving headmaster 1848–87 (see page 22). He left £100 to buy oranges for annual distribution and the first such event took place on 13 April 1911. The school closed in 1967 but the custom is still maintained at Swinemoor Primary School.

Section Seven

THE PASTURES

*The Westwood, York Road. The 504-acre Westwood is Beverley's best known and most
frequented common pasture. All that remains of the great wood which once covered the area
is Burton Bushes, the outer fringe opposite the racecourse. The Westwood is under the
control of twelve Pasture Masters elected annually by the Freemen of Beverley.*

Fishwick's Mill or Butt Close Mill, pre-1861. One of the five mills formerly on the Westwood, it was a wooden post-mill (one which was moved round a central post set into its base so that it caught the wind) erected in 1761. Its demolition in 1861 was followed by a violent protest by Beverley freemen in which they claimed that the mill house had been built on pasture land which belonged to them.

Westwood Far Mill or Black Mill. This mill, which had a brick tower, was built in 1802. The working parts were damaged by fire and it was dismantled in 1868.

The Union or Anti Mill. A mill with a radical history; it was built in 1799 by the Union Mill Society which operated it as a co-operative in competition with private mill owners accused of over-charging. It went out of use in about 1890. The upper part was dismantled and the lower section is now incorporated into the clubhouse of the Beverley and East Riding Golf Club.

Chalk Pit Mill. Situated just off the Westwood on the Walkington Road, its function was to grind chalk into whiting. The upper part of the mill was dismantled around 1890 and it now forms part of ECC Calcium Carbonates, whiting manufacturers.

The Westwood flooded in the 1912 cloudburst. The two-hour storm began at 2 p.m. on 24 July and a torrent of water poured down from the Westwood, forcing inhabitants of Willow Grove to seek safety upstairs. It alarmed some so much that they ordered cabs to evacuate their children (see also page 24).

A neatherd's cottage, Westwood Road. These Gothic-style lodges were built in 1856 by the Pasture Masters to enable the occupants to control access to the Westwood and to keep a watchful eye on animals grazing there. The vehicle appears to be a canvas-covered wagon of the type used by carriers from the villages who travelled regularly to Beverley markets.

Temporary entrance erected for the Yorkshire Show held on the Westwood 10–12 August 1909.

Avro 504 aircraft, the Westwood, c. 1920. Flying was a fashionable sport and flights were offered to local people brave enough to try a new experience. During the First World War a large area of the Westwood was used as an aerodrome by the Royal Flying Corps.

Section Eight

HISTORIC INNS

Sun Inn, Flemingate, c. 1880. The timber-framed building, one of the few still visible in Beverley, dates from the sixteenth century. It might even be earlier but it has been Victorianized. In 1994 it underwent renovation and restoration and was renamed the Tap and Spile.

The Foresters Arms, Beckside. A nineteenth-century building, formerly called the Cock and Bottle, it was demolished and replaced by the present one in mock-Tudor style. Inns often have a complicated history, undergoing alteration or complete rebuilding as circumstances change. A landlord would also sometimes take the name of an inn with him when he moved to new premises.

The Valiant Soldier, Norwood, c. 1900. Here it has a mock-Tudor appearance. It is, however, much older than this fashionable turn of the century style would suggest, dating from the late seventeenth or early eighteenth century. Georgian traffic congestion at the Assembly Rooms caused the section at the Walkergate corner to be lopped off, in 1811, for road widening, leaving the inn with its present asymmetrical façade. For a time it was known as the Holderness, but this name was taken over by the Blue Boar, Toll Gavel in 1829 (see page 27). The houses to the left of the inn later became the site of N. Healey's butcher's shop and the Clock Garage.

The White Horse Inn, Hengate. Built in the late seventeenth century, though parts may be earlier, it still has its original Georgian shutters and, although renovated in more recent times, retains much of the authentic atmosphere of an old inn. The white horse now above the front door is a modern replacement of the one shown in this photograph, a rocking horse which had belonged to Richard Whiteing, an architect, who lived opposite. The shop on the far left has been demolished.

Section Nine

THE SOCIAL SCENE

Beverley's own movie mogul, 1935. Ernest Symmons (left) ran the Picture Playhouse and made Beverley's own newsreels. Here he is at work on the film The Villain in the Wood. *It was made to aid the restoration of the roof of St Mary's Church.*
Canon T.H. Tardrew, the well-known vicar of St Mary's, a popular preacher and a great Beverley character, is in the centre. The other man is unknown.

Beverley Inner Wheel Club charter day, 13 February 1950. Beverley has a long tradition as a place of thriving social, political and charitable groups. This photograph was taken in the ballroom behind the Beverley Arms. The president is Mrs C.F. Deans, the secretary Mrs Edna Ward, and other well-known Beverlonians on the photograph include Mrs Bessie Watts, Mrs Edna Dunning, Mrs Betty Sedgwick, Mrs Thelma Symmons, Mrs 'Bubbles' Hodgson, Mrs Ralph Lindsay, Mrs Frank Edwards, Mrs J. Huzzard and Mrs Nancy Care.

The Borough Council, *c.* 1900. The members are leaving the Guildhall in Register Square. The occasion has not been identified but it could be in connection with the death of Queen Victoria and the accession of Edward VII in 1901. As Lord Roberts Road has not been opened the group take the Butcher Row route to the Minster. The mayor, who is wearing a bowler hat, appears to be James E. Elwell who was in office from 1900 to 1902.

James E. Elwell, Mayor, North Bar Within, *c.* 1900. J.E. Elwell, a distinguished wood carver, was the father of F.W. Elwell, the even more famous artist. Behind him, in a bowler hat, is Harry Wray, solicitor and member of the Borough Council.

'Beverley through the ages', 10 July 1937. A pageant celebrating the 1000th anniversary of King Athelstan's re-founding the Minster as a collegiate church, this was the most ambitious civic event of the inter-war years. The procession is passing through North Bar. On the left are the Tudor-style buildings, erected 1892–4 by James E. Elwell. He ran his wood-carving business from no. 4, the tallest building in the group.

F.W. Elwell in fancy dress, 1937. Fred Elwell, the artist, was a man of some dignity. On this occasion he is dressed in Tudor costume and carrying the flag, presumably having been 'persuaded' to play his part.

AROUND THE MINSTER

Beverley Minster from the north-west. All the surrounding impediments have been removed

by the artist to enable the church to be seen in all its glory.

Hauling 'Great John' into the south-west tower of the Minster, 18 February 1902. This new bell, by Taylor of Loughborough, replaced one which was discordant. In the background on the left are the older houses of St John Street which incorporate parts of buildings once part of the Minster complex. On the right are late Victorian houses.

Nearly there! The bell rests in position before hauling up the south-west tower. Because of its weight (7 tons), 'Great John' is installed in the south-west tower and the peal in the north-east. This is believed to be a unique arrangement.

Minster churchyard. This bell appears to be different from 'Great John'. It might be one of the bells installed in 1900 or 1901.

Fred Elwell, RA, painting the Minster and the Hall Garth Inn, *c.* 1927. He has set up his easel in the field to the south-west. This was formerly occupied by buildings connected with the Minster when it was a collegiate church. The Hall Garth Inn was demolished in 1958.

Minster chancel screen. The screen, designed by Sir Gilbert Scott, was carved by James E. Elwell's firm and dedicated on 4 October 1880 to replace the eighteenth-century stone screen removed in 1875. This photograph was taken before the installation of the new organ case in 1916.

Unveiling the statue of Queen Victoria, 22 June 1897. As part of the Diamond Jubilee celebrations the Mayoress, Mrs G. Whiteing, unveiled the statue on the west front of the Minster. The ceremony was photographed by J. Butler. Canon H.E. Nolloth, vicar from 1880 to 1921, had inaugurated the scheme for filling the niches with statues.

Beverley Minster from the south-west with the Hall Garth Inn to the right. This view conveys well the atmosphere of a town which had the countryside only a few steps away.

St John Street before removal of the Minster churchyard wall (left) in 1905 (see page 13).

Minster Moorgate. In the background are the western towers of the Minster. When it was a pre-Reformation collegiate church senior officials probably occupied premises in this street: the existing houses are now mainly of nineteenth-century date. Minster National Infants School on the right was built in 1886, closed in 1972 and is now converted into a house.

131–3 Keldgate. These last two authentic Beverley cottages were demolished in 1979.

Gardens of the former Dominican Friary, 1956. Still inhabited as three separate houses, the Friary was sold to Armstrong Patents Co. Ltd in 1960 and is now restored and in use as a youth hostel. This section of the Friary, which survives, was probably the dormitory and library.

Acknowledgements

Many people have, directly and indirectly, knowingly and unknowingly, contributed to this book. A collection of photographs is built up over a long period, and a great debt is owed to all who, over the years, have given copies of illustrations from their own collections. In the absence of a detailed catalogue showing the provenance of all photographs it is impossible to thank by name all those who have helped to make this book possible, but the gratitude of the authors is no less sincere.

All historians, too, benefit from the work of their predecessors, and Beverley has been particularly fortunate in the number of researchers and writers who have explored so many aspects of the town's history and contributed to our deeper knowledge and understanding of its past. The authors are only too happy to acknowledge their indebtedness to all who have previously published their work and made so much valuable information freely available. Nor would they wish to forget those who are not published authors but have been so helpful in providing information and advice on points of difficulty.

BRITAIN IN OLD PHOTOGRAPHS

To order any of these titles please telephone Littlehampton Book Services on 01903 721596

ALDERNEY

Alderney: A Second Selection, *B Bonnard*

BEDFORDSHIRE

Bedfordshire at Work, *N Lutt*

BERKSHIRE

Maidenhead, *M Hayles & D Hedges*
Around Maidenhead, *M Hayles & B Hedges*
Reading, *P Southerton*
Reading: A Second Selection, *P Southerton*
Sandhurst and Crowthorne, *K Dancy*
Around Slough, *J Hunter & K Hunter*
Around Thatcham, *P Allen*
Around Windsor, *B Hedges*

BUCKINGHAMSHIRE

Buckingham and District, *R Cook*
High Wycombe, *R Goodearl*
Around Stony Stratford, *A Lambert*

CHESHIRE

Cheshire Railways, *M Hitches*
Chester, *S Nichols*

CLWYD

Clwyd Railways, *M Hitches*

CLYDESDALE

Clydesdale, *Lesmahagow Parish Historical Association*

CORNWALL

Cornish Coast, *T Bowden*
Falmouth, *P Gilson*
Lower Fal, *P Gilson*
Around Padstow, *M McCarthy*
Around Penzance, *J Holmes*
Penzance and Newlyn, *J Holmes*
Around Truro, *A Lyne*
Upper Fal, *P Gilson*

CUMBERLAND

Cockermouth and District, *J Bernard Bradbury*
Keswick and the Central Lakes, *J Marsh*
Around Penrith, *F Boyd*
Around Whitehaven, *H Fancy*

DERBYSHIRE

Derby, *D Buxton*
Around Matlock, *D Barton*

DEVON

Colyton and Seaton, *T Gosling*
Dawlish and Teignmouth, *G Gosling*
Devon Aerodromes, *K Saunders*
Exeter, *P Thomas*
Exmouth and Budleigh Salterton, *T Gosling*
From Haldon to Mid-Dartmoor, *T Hall*
Honiton and the Otter Valley, *J Yallop*
Around Kingsbridge, *K Tanner*
Around Seaton and Sidmouth, *T Gosling*
Seaton, AxMinster and Lyme Regis, *T Gosling*

DORSET

Around Blandford Forum, *B Cox*
Bournemouth, *M Colman*
Bridport and the Bride Valley, *J Burrell & S Humphries*
Dorchester, *T Gosling*
Around Gillingham, *P Crocker*

DURHAM

Darlington, *G Flynn*
Darlington: A Second Selection, *G Flynn*
Durham People, *M Richardson*
Houghton-le-Spring and Hetton-le-Hole, *K Richardson*
Houghton-le-Spring and Hetton-le-Hole:
  A Second Selection, *K Richardson*
Sunderland, *S Miller & B Bell*
Teesdale, *D Coggins*
Teesdale: A Second Selection, *P Raine*
Weardale, *J Crosby*
Weardale: A Second Selection, *J Crosby*

DYFED

Aberystwyth and North Ceredigion,
  Dyfed Cultural Services Dept
Haverfordwest, *Dyfed Cultural Services Dept*
Upper Tywi Valley, *Dyfed Cultural Services Dept*

ESSEX

Around Grays, *B Evans*

GLOUCESTERSHIRE

Along the Avon from Stratford to Tewkesbury, *J Jeremiah*
Cheltenham: A Second Selection, *R Whiting*
Cheltenham at War, *P Gill*
Cirencester, *J Welsford*
Around Cirencester, *E Cuss & P Griffiths*
Forest, The, *D Mullin*
Gloucester, *J Voyce*
Around Gloucester, *A Sutton*
Gloucester: From the Walwin Collection, *J Voyce*
North Cotswolds, *D Viner*
Severn Vale, *A Sutton*
Stonehouse to Painswick, *A Sutton*
Stroud and the Five Valleys, *S Gardiner & L Padin*
Stroud and the Five Valleys: A Second Selection,
  S Gardiner & L Padin
Stroud's Golden Valley, *S Gardiner & L Padin*
Stroudwater and Thames & Severn Canals,
  E Cuss & S Gardiner
Stroudwater and Thames & Severn Canals: A Second
  Selection, *E Cuss & S Gardiner*
Tewkesbury and the Vale of Gloucester, *C Hilton*
Thornbury to Berkeley, *J Hudson*
Uley, Dursley and Cam, *A Sutton*
Wotton-under-Edge to Chipping Sodbury, *A Sutton*

GWYNEDD

Anglesey, *M Hitches*
Gwynedd Railways, *M Hitches*
Around Llandudno, *M Hitches*
Vale of Conwy, *M Hitches*

HAMPSHIRE

Gosport, *J Sadden*
Portsmouth, *P Rogers & D Francis*

HEREFORDSHIRE

Herefordshire, *A Sandford*

HERTFORDSHIRE

Barnet, *I Norrie*
Hitchin, *A Fleck*
St Albans, *S Mullins*
Stevenage, *M Appleton*

ISLE OF MAN

The Tourist Trophy, *B Snelling*

ISLE OF WIGHT

Newport, *D Parr*
Around Ryde, *D Parr*

JERSEY

Jersey: A Third Selection, *R Lempriere*

KENT

Bexley, *M Scott*
Broadstairs and St Peter's, *J Whyman*
Bromley, Keston and Hayes, *M Scott*
Canterbury: A Second Selection, *D Butler*
Chatham and Gillingham, *P MacDougall*
Chatham Dockyard, *P MacDougall*
Deal, *J Broady*
Early Broadstairs and St Peter's, *B Wootton*
East Kent at War, *D Collyer*
Eltham, *J Kennett*
Folkestone: A Second Selection, *A Taylor & E Rooney*
Goudhurst to Tenterden, *A Guilmant*
Gravesend, *R Hiscock*
Around Gravesham, *R Hiscock & D Grierson*
Herne Bay, *J Hawkins*
Lympne Airport, *D Collyer*
Maidstone, *I Hales*
Margate, *R Clements*
RAF Hawkinge, *R Humphreys*
RAF Manston, *RAF Manston History Club*
RAF Manston: A Second Selection,
  RAF Manston History Club
Ramsgate and Thanet Life, *D Perkins*
Romney Marsh, *E Carpenter*
Sandwich, *C Wanostrocht*
Around Tonbridge, *C Bell*
Tunbridge Wells, *M Rowlands & I Beavis*
Tunbridge Wells: A Second Selection,
  M Rowlands & I Beavis
Around Whitstable, *C Court*
Wingham, Adisham and Littlebourne, *M Crane*

LANCASHIRE

Around Barrow-in-Furness, *J Garbutt & J Marsh*
Blackpool, *C Rothwell*
Bury, *J Hudson*
Chorley and District, *J Smith*
Fleetwood, *C Rothwell*
Heywood, *J Hudson*
Around Kirkham, *C Rothwell*
Lancashire North of the Sands, *J Garbutt & J Marsh*
Around Lancaster, *S Ashworth*
Lytham St Anne's, *C Rothwell*
North Fylde, *C Rothwell*
Radcliffe, *J Hudson*
Rossendale, *B Moore & N Dunnachie*

LEICESTERSHIRE

Around Ashby-de-la-Zouch, *K Hillier*
Charnwood Forest, *I Keil, W Humphrey & D Wix*
Leicester, *D Burton*
Leicester: A Second Selection, *D Burton*
Melton Mowbray, *T Hickman*
Around Melton Mowbray, *T Hickman*
River Soar, *D Wix, P Shacklock & I Keil*
Rutland, *T Clough*
Vale of Belvoir, *T Hickman*
Around the Welland Valley, *S Mastoris*

LINCOLNSHIRE

Grimsby, *J Tierney*
Around Grimsby, *J Tierney*
Grimsby Docks, *J Tierney*
Lincoln, *D Cuppleditch*